Northwest Coast Indians

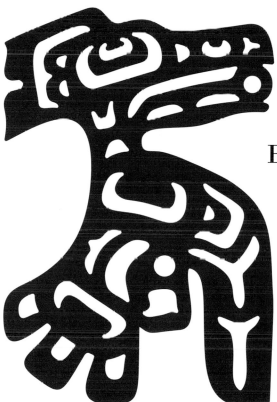

By Mira Bartók and
Christine Ronan

 GoodYearBooks

An Imprint of ScottForesman
A Division of HarperCollinsPublishers

Alaska

Canada

•Seattle

United States

The Northwest Coast Indians live in the Northwest United States, Canada, and Alaska.

They live along the Pacific Ocean
near rain forests. Many animals,
birds, and fish live there too.

Some Indian people hunt and fish
for their food. They give thanks to
these animals in many ways.

Making giant totem poles is a
way to thank the animals.

Raven   Thunderbird

They make animal designs
called crests.

8

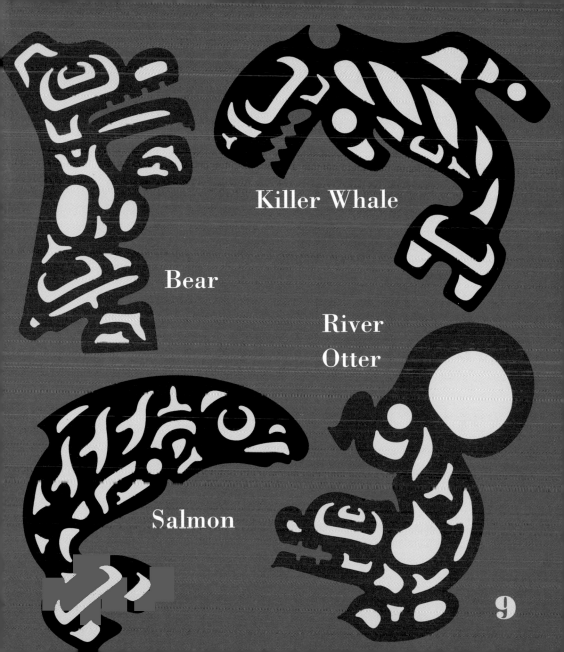

Killer Whale

Bear

River
Otter

Salmon

9

The Indians
believe both
animals and
crests have
special
powers.
Here is a
killer whale
crest.

10

Here is
a bear
crest.

During ceremonies the Indians thank the animals by singing and telling stories.

They drum
and dance.
Sometimes
they even
dance sitting
down!

These people are going to a
ceremony called a Potlatch.
They are beating their drums and
singing as a message of friendship.

The Potlatch is a ceremony where people give many gifts and learn about respect and sharing.

All of these traditions—art, stories,
and ceremonies—are passed down to
children by parents and grandparents.